anythi...

II0633379

WHAT DECADE DO YOU BELONG IN?

By Brooke Rowe

Published in the United States of America by Cherry Lake Publishing
Ann Arbor, Michigan
www.cherrylakepublishing.com

Reading Adviser: Marla Conn, ReadAbility, Inc.
Book Designer: Melinda Millward

Photo Credits: © William Perugini/Shutterstock.com, back cover, 4; © monkeybusinessimages/Thinkstock.com, back cover, 4; ©Massonstock | iStockphoto, cover, 1; ©IPGGutenbergUKLtd/Thinkstock, 6; ©Volt Collection/Shutterstock Images, 6; ©InkkStudios | iStockphoto, 7; ©i4lcocl2 /Shutterstock Images, 7; ©LeviQ/Shutterstock Images, 8; ©Oleg Gekman/Shutterstock Images, 8; ©Viorel Sima/Shutterstock Images, 9; ©Zurijeta/Shutterstock Images, 9; ©blvdone/Shutterstock Images, 10; ©BrAt82/Shutterstock Images, 10; ©OlegDoroshin/Shutterstock Images, 11; ©Giuseppe Costantino/Shutterstock Images, 11; ©Apirut Siri/Shutterstock Images, 12; ©luminaimages/Shutterstock Images, 12; ©Evgeniya Porechenskaya/Shutterstock Images, 13; ©Rommel Canlas/Shutterstock Images, 13; ©Kamira/Shutterstock Images, 14; ©My Good Images/Shutterstock Images, 14; ©vm2002/Shutterstock Images, 15; ©Michaelpuche/Shutterstock Images, 15; ©AS Food studio/Shutterstock Images, 16; ©ilolab/Shutterstock Images, 16; ©El Nariz/Shutterstock Images, 17; ©MSPhotographic/Shutterstock Images, 17; ©ixer/Shutterstock Images, 18; ©Jezper/Shutterstock Images, 18; ©shannonstent/iStockphoto, 19; ©mikolajn/Shutterstock Images, 19; ©TCreativeMedia/Shutterstock Images, 20; ©Zuzule/Shutterstock Images, 20; ©Reflex Life/Shutterstock Images, 21; ©ilterriorm/Shutterstock Images, 21; ©mimagephotography/Shutterstock Images, 22; ©Ditty_about_summer/Shutterstock Images, 22; ©vita khorzhevska/Shutterstock Images, 23; ©Andrey Armyagov/Shutterstock Images, 23; © Pedxer/CanStock, 24; ©Africa Studio/Shutterstock Images, 24; ©Anetlanda/Thinkstock, 25; ©Giuseppe Costantino/Shutterstock Images, 25; ©michaeljung/Shutterstock Images, 26; ©Katsiaryna Pakhomava/Shutterstock Images, 26; ©Dean Drobot/Shutterstock Images, 27; ©Joe_Potato | iStockphoto, 27; ©SvetlanaSF/Shutterstock Images, 28; ©Lorcel/Shutterstock Images, 28; ©Racheal Grazias/Shutterstock Images, 29; ©Linda Moon/Shutterstock Images, 29; ©mandygodbehear | iStockphoto, 30; ©Dudarev Mikhail/Shutterstock Images, 30; ©mandygodbehear/Shutterstock Images, 31; ©lassedesignen/Shutterstock Images, 31

Graphic Element Credits: © Silhouette Lover/Shutterstock Images, back cover, multiple interior pages; © Arevik/Shutterstock Images, back cover, multiple interior pages; © tukkki/Shutterstock Images, multiple interior pages; © paprika/Shutterstock Images, 24

45th Parallel Press is an imprint of Cherry Lake Publishing.

Library of Congress Cataloging-in-Publication Data

Rowe, Brooke, author.
    What decade do you belong in? / Brooke Rowe.
pages cm. — (Best quiz ever)
Includes bibliographical references and index.
ISBN 978-1-63470-508-0 (hardcover) — ISBN 978-1-63470-568-4 (pdf) —
ISBN 978-1-63470-628-5 (pbk.) — ISBN 978-1-63470-688-9 (ebook)
1. Civilization, Modern—Miscellanea—Juvenile literature. 2. History—Miscellanea—
Juvenile literature. 3. Personality tests—Juvenile literature. I. Title.
CB426.R69 2016
909—dc23   2015026871

Printed in the United States of America
Corporate Graphics

Table of Contents

Introduction

Hey! Welcome to the Best Quiz Ever series. This is a book. Duh. But it's also a pretty awesome quiz. Don't worry. It's not about math. Or history. Or anything you might get graded on. Snooze.

This is a quiz all about YOU.

To take the Best Quiz Ever:

Answer honestly!
Keep track of your answers. But don't write in the book!
(Hint: Make a copy of this handy chart.)
Don't see the answer you want? Pick the closest one.
Take it alone. Take it with friends!
Have fun! Obviously.

Question 1 _____   Question 7 _____

Question 2 _____   Question 8 _____

Question 3 _____   Question 9 _____

Question 4 _____   Question 10 _____

Question 5 _____   Question 11 _____

Question 6 _____   Question 12 _____

To get a copy of this activity, visit
www.cherrylakepublishing.com/activities.

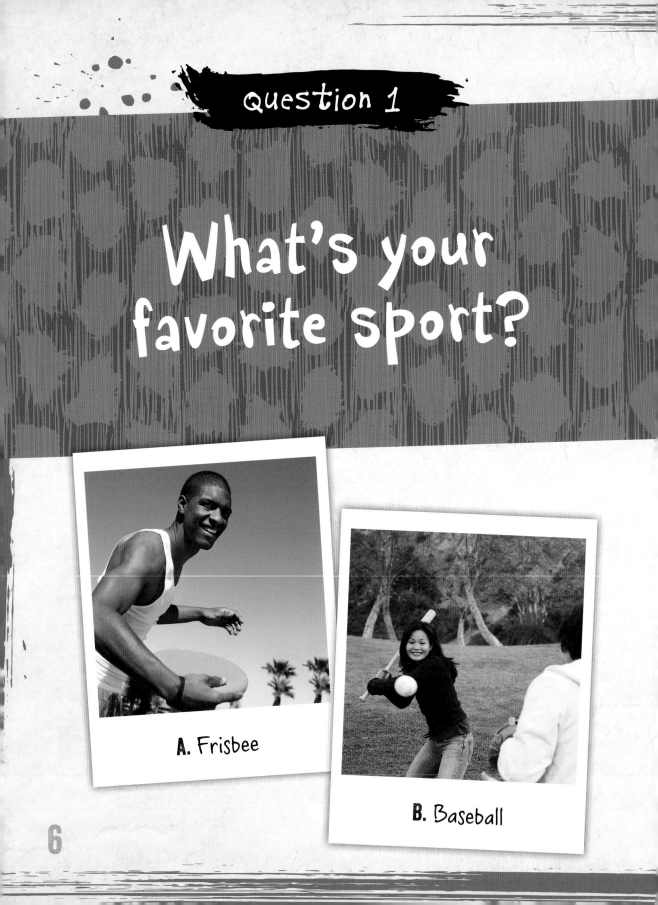

What's your favorite sport?

A. Frisbee

B. Baseball

6

C. Football

D. Anything in the X Games!

Did you know?
The first X Games were held in Rhode Island in 1995.

Who would you love to hang out with?

A. Bob Dylan

B. Lewis and Clark

C. Bon Jovi

D. Stephen Hawking

Did you know?

Lewis and Clark traveled 8,000 miles (12,875 kilometers) of wilderness in America's west. The trip took three years.

Question 3

What kind of phone do you have?

A. Mom's old iPhone

B. I'm not into smartphones

C. New Android

D. I'm saving up for the Next Big Thing

Did you know?

Experts think the next generation of smartphones will be super thin—and flexible!

What's on your head?

A. Flower crown

B. Knit hat

C. A rockin' do

D. 3-D virtual
reality glasses

Did you know?
Singer Lana Del Rey made flower crowns
popular again in 2014.

You couldn't live without this invention:

A. Calculator

B. The wheel

C. Ice cream maker

D. Internet

Did you know?

The first Saturday in February is known as Ice Cream for Breakfast Day.

You're at the food court—what's for lunch?

A. Tofu and veggies

B. Burger and fries

16

C. Pizza and bread sticks

D. Pie à la mode

Did you know?

The community of Pie Town, New Mexico, is named for an apple pie bakery that was there in the 1920s.

Bad news.
What is it?

A. Global warming

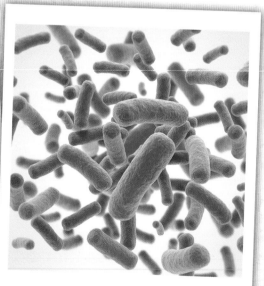

B. Disease **outbreak**

C. Tsunami

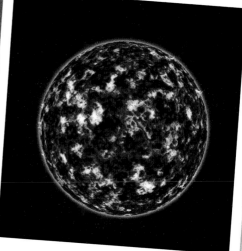

D. Solar storm

Did you know?

A geomagnetic storm, or solar storm, is activity on the sun that interferes with Earth's magnetic field.

You got a puppy for your birthday! What's her name?

A. Janis

B. Annie

C. Punky

D. Amidala

Did you know?

The Puppy Bowl airs on Animal Planet during the halftime of the Super Bowl. It features puppies playing together. The 2015 Puppy Bowl had 2.7 million viewers.

What's your personal motto?

A. Peace and love

B. Not all who wander are lost

C. Only the **meek** get pinched. The bold survive.

D. To infinity and beyond!

Did you know?

"Not all who wander are lost" is a line in a poem written by J. R. R. Tolkien for The Lord of the Rings.

What accessory is on your back-to-school list

A. Mood ring

B. Backpack

C. New Jeggings

D. Apple Watch

Did you know?

The largest backpack ever made measured 39 feet (11.8 meters) high and 30 feet (9.1 m) wide. This world's record was made August 6, 2015, in Russia.

Your best friend is starting a band. You're playing:

A. Acoustic guitar

B. Harmonica

C. Keyboard

D. Plastic bucket drums

Did you know?
Drummer Rick Allen, from the band Def Leppard,
lost his left arm in a car accident in 1985.
He still plays drums, with one arm.

The best class trip would be to:

A. San Francisco

B. Yellowstone National Park

C. Six Flags

D. Camp Kennedy Space Center

Did you know?

In Yellowstone National Park, your chances of being **mauled** by a bear are 1 in 2.1 million.

Solutions

You're done! Now you tally your score. Add up your As, Bs, Cs, and Ds. What letter do you have the most of? BTW, if you have a tie, you're a little bit of both.

As: 1960s

Far out—you're a flower child! You have a free spirit. You're creative and laid-back. You think it's important to make the world a better place. You love listening to groovy music with your friends. But you aren't afraid to stand up for your beliefs. You're stoked about everything life has to offer. You belong in the 1960s. Right on!

Bs: 1840s

You have some real true grit. You definitely would have survived the Oregon Trail! And been first in line for the gold rush. You love exploring new places. Especially places NO ONE has been before. You'd always rather be outside. You have a practical style. You don't need technology to get through your day. You're down-to-earth. You belong in the 1840s!

Cs: 1980s

Gnarly! You are SO totally from the '80s. You love things big and bright. Your music. Your clothes. Your hair. Your personality. Your friends are majorly important to you. You love spending weekends with them at the beach or mall. In fact, shopping is one of your fave activities. You usually go with the flow. And you're almost always happy.

Ds: The Future

You are beyond. Way too smart for yesterday or today! You belong in the future. Technology is your game. If there's a new trend, you are the first to know. And you're always thinking outside the box. WAY outside the box. Some think you're a little strange. But you're destined to be an inventor. Or a tech CEO. Whatever you do, you'll always be thinking ahead. The future is NOW!

Glossary

acoustic (uh-KOO-stik) sound that is not charged by electrical devices

mauled (MAWLD) attacked and injured by an animal

meek (MEEK) lacking spirit

outbreak (OUT-brake) a sudden increase of something unpleasant

tsunami (tsu-NAH-mee) a very large, destructive sea wave

Index